Whoso Findeth a Wife

Revised and Expanded

Dene Ward

DeWard
for your journey

For my mother, Hilda Ayers, who taught me how.

Whoso Findeth A Wife...

Many years ago, Connie Adams asked me to write a few articles for the periodical *Searching the Scriptures*. I had known brother Adams since I was a child in Orlando where he preached for the Pine Hills congregation and where my family attended. I was honored that he asked me to write for him, and for a few months wrote a regular column on being a wife. Later those same articles ran in another periodical called *Contents of the Weaker Vessel*. Still later I edited them and added another article and some questions for classroom use.

All these years later I pulled out one of those workbooks and discovered a host of typographical errors, including errant scriptures. I had also honed my writing skills by then, and over the years had gained far more experience as a wife. Here and there I was embarrassed at what I had written. So I pulled the remaining books out of circulation and began a serious rewrite. I completely deleted one article, heavily edited the rest, and wrote four completely new ones.

It also became apparent to me that by limiting this to a women's Bible class I was missing some people who may need it the most. I want this to be something any woman can pick up and read for her own edification whether she has a class to attend or not. I can't help myself though, it seems my inborn nature to teach. So I have added a short list of questions "for thought or discussion" after each article in case an individual would like to use it for personal study, but also so a group could use it in a class if they want to. Each student can furnish their own small notebook for answers and notes. I hope all of this will make it appealing to more people, and perhaps a useful addition to a wedding shower gift or something a mother would want to give her newly engaged daughter.

Despite the opinion of today's woman, who believes that being a wife is so simple she must have something *real* to do with her life, it is not that easy. Christians, too, have fallen into the notion that there is nothing to it. Rather than studying what God has said with open and understanding minds, we have accepted the stereotype handed down by society, family, even older Christians. Whereas the older training the younger is scriptural procedure, if their training comes only from subjective experience and opinion, and not from the word of God, each generation gradually drifts further from the original. Too often culture has a way of sneaking into our thinking, and whereas the Scriptures suit all cultures, not all cultures suit the Scriptures. I can be a modern woman and still be a Christian, but only if I accept God's word in its entirety and alter my behavior as necessary.

Yet that isn't the way it always works. Countless numbers read Ephesians 5 and 1 Peter 3 in every ladies' Bible class, and still do not recognize their own failures as wives. We have brainwashed ourselves into believing that because we can quote these pet scriptures, are willing to say, "My husband is the head of the house," and at least follow the norm in the church, we are good wives. No wonder we find it so easy! Paul warned the Corinthians about using something other than the scriptures to measure their righteousness (2 Cor 10.12). One can always find someone worse than she, if she looks low enough.

John teaches us that saying and doing are two entirely different things: "[My] little children, let us not love in word, neither with the tongue; but in deed and truth" (1 John 3.18). The same women who quote scripture will ridicule their husbands to others, try to deceive them and think nothing of it, and make pronouncements about what those men will and will not do "in my house." The friends and neighbors, who see us everyday, as opposed to we who blind ourselves to our behavior may have an entirely different opinion about who runs our homes, and the state of our marriage.

No matter what our culture says, we cannot be Christians without accepting the New Testament as our guide for living, and Ephesians 5, Colossians 3, and 1 Peter 3 are rich passages for us to turn to. But if we do not learn how to apply them, their benefit is lost. Romans 15.4 gives the Christian the authority to search out the Old Testament, "things written aforetime," for other clues to what God meant a wife to be. She will find there many simple metaphors that will give her both a broader perspective and a deeper insight into the job she has before her. It is a few of these passages we will look at in this study.

> *Whoso findeth a wife, findeth a good thing, and obtaineth favor of Jehovah.*
>
> Proverbs 18.22

Dene Ward

August 2014

1. A Good Thing

Whoso findeth a wife findeth a good thing. (Prov 18.22)

Does one become a good thing by simply saying, "I do?" In other words, is every wife a good thing? There might be a point to this we overlook. Because we know the answer is "no," we add a few words to the scripture. "Whoso findeth a wife *might have* found a good thing." But that is not what it says! A wife is something he has to look for whereas women who want to marry are a dime a dozen. We are also told that the worthy woman (wife) is hard to find (Prov 31.10). Perhaps the point is that not every married woman *deserves* to be called a wife.

There was an era when society cast a blind eye on a man who had both a wife and a mistress. Yet even then, most decent women would have been insulted to be asked to be a mistress instead of a wife. It was an honor to be a man's wife, and one recognized the responsibilities it laid upon her in behavior and management of the home. You've seen those old movies just like I have. "You don't think I'm good enough to marry!" the courtesan screams at the two-timing husband.

"Good enough to be a wife," shows that the position was held in honor, even if not every man treated it that way.

And nowadays? It has become more important to assert and indulge *self.* A woman may keep her own name, or add his as an appendage to it. She may have a career, which he must realize takes precedence over the home they planned to make together, and which may even take precedence over his career. She may farm out their children to someone else to raise, very often a stranger whose values may or may not reflect theirs. And in many cases, she may not even marry him. Why bother when society doesn't even seem to care any more either? Once again we see that attitude: "What's the big deal with being a wife? I need something *real* to do."

Management of the home has taken a bad rap. When my husband tells people, "I have no idea what's what. She takes care of everything," I don't find it a bit demeaning. Isn't that what women say they want these days, some recognition and appreciation for the skills they use every day? My husband comes to me when he runs out of toothpaste, when he can't find his favorite jeans, and when he needs the receipt for the shoes whose sole separated after just a month's wear. I am the one who keeps supplies stocked, sorts and files the sales slips, and knows that he wore a hole in the seat of those jeans far too large to patch with anything but a quilt. I am the one who knows which bill is due when, and whether we can afford that new chainsaw he thinks he needs. That's exactly what the word means in 1 Timothy 5.14, the younger widow is to remarry and **manage** the home—*oikodespoteo*—to manage [as a steward under a head], very much like a store manager under an owner. It carries a lot of responsibility and delegated authority. "It is required in stewards that they be found faithful" (1 Cor 4.2).

But that isn't the half of it. What makes this wife a good thing is that he can trust her. "She does him good and not evil all the days of her life" (Prov 31.12). The modern woman is too worried about doing for herself to do for him and their home. I have heard far too many of them whine about needing "me time," even Christians. Jesus said to save your life you need to lose it in service to others. We will never find "me time" if that's all we ever look for. To save your life, you must lose it.

Doing him good all the days of your life means whether he deserves it or not, whether he can do for you or not. I watched my mother care for my father for twelve years before he died, day and night, sacrificing her own health and well-being, even though those final three or four years he had no idea who she was. She remembered the vows she made, not just to him, but before God as well, sixty plus years before. If anyone deserved to be called a wife, she did.

It is one thing to say, "I am this man's wife." It is another to be his wife. We should count it an honor to be our man's wife. Griping about the man or the job is not the way it's done.

A worthy woman who can find? …The heart of her husband trusts in her, and he shall have no lack of gain. She does him good and not evil all the days of her life. … She opens her mouth with wisdom; and the law of kindness is on her tongue. She looks well to the ways of her household, And eats not the bread of idleness.

Proverbs 31.10–12, 26–27

For Thought or Discussion

1. "Good" is one of those words we use so much that it has lost its meaning. In fact, in today's world of hyperbolic language it can even mean "mediocre." Find the original meaning of the Hebrew word *tob*, and other passages where its use can help explain its meaning.

2. The word is used in both Proverbs 18.22 and 31.12. What "good" might the "good thing" do for her husband all the days of her life? What if he dies first?

3. Can this include "good" that he might not like or appreciate?

4. Find instances in the Scriptures of wives doing "good" for their husbands.

5. What attitudes and behaviors would doing him "good" necessarily exclude?

2. The Fruitful Vine

In Psalm 128.3 the woman is called the fruitful vine. In the Psalm this refers primarily to bearing children, but it can also be true in other areas in which the wife acts as a producer for her husband.

The most important thing a homemaker produces is exactly what her title says—a home. Unfortunately, homemaking often has a bad name. The woman at home is portrayed as a leech on her husband's arm—always consuming and never producing. In this portrait, she is sitting in her easy chair, a television in front of her, a telephone on one side, romance novels and sales catalogues on the other—or maybe a computer monitor or iPhone these days? On the one day a week she is not reading, gossiping, or staring, she is out spending her husband's hard-earned money on more clothes, a shampoo and set, and a basket full of overpriced convenience food. The beds are never made. The clothes may be washed, but one always has to pick through the laundry basket for clean underwear. Dinner varies from Chef-Boy-Ar-Dee to Stouffer's, depending upon the occasion. The children care for themselves, coming and going as they please. She does not know if they have done their homework or Bible lessons; she has no idea if they are being taught evolution, situation ethics, humanism, or any other atheistic -ism. If her children were kidnapped, she wouldn't know what they were last wearing, when they left the house, with whom, or in what direction—she sleeps in, you see.

That is our image, ladies, and some of it is our fault. We started believing our detractors when they told us how unfulfilling our lives were. They asked us if we work, and instead of proudly saying, "Of course, I work; I'm a homemaker," we hung our heads and muttered an apology about being "just a housewife." Titus 2.5 calls the woman a worker at home. We have been so busy emphasizing the "at home," that we have forgotten to emphasize "worker." No, we do not punch a time clock, but that makes it more difficult, not less. We have to make ourselves take the time and do the work. We are on call 24 hours a day, 7 days a week—no holidays.

It takes as many hours to stretch a dollar (gardening, canning, sewing, coupon clipping, comparison shopping, baking from scratch) as it does to earn one. It takes more time to read and discuss a Bible story that it does to plop a child in front of a television set. It takes extra time to read up on humanism and monitor our children's schoolwork for its insidious signs; then it takes old-fashioned nerve to speak up about it. It takes more self-discipline and creativity to be a homemaker than any other career in the world!

But it is a most rewarding calling if it is handled as God intended. When one truly produces a home, people notice, not just because the housework is done, but because the atmosphere of the home is carried everywhere with the family members. A haven, peaceful and secure—the place you run to not from—that is a home.

The fruitful vine lives to produce. She is never resentful or regretful. When we do as Titus 2.4 says and learn to love our husbands (not just "fall" in love) and to love our children, the homes we produce for them will show our love because all the work we do is for them. The fruitful vine asks nothing in return from those who pick her grapes. Because the fruit is so plenteous and good, her loved ones shower her with care and attention.

And remember this: in today's world, where women often need to work outside the home, God has not given you a pass on this one. He still expects you to be "a fruitful vine." My choices never outweigh God's plan.

What kind of fruit are you producing, ladies? Is it scarce? Tough? Undersized? Seedy? Sour? Does it come like a fortune cookie with a little message inside: "(Sigh) and after all I've done for you...."

It takes extra effort to be a fruitful vine. Let's get to work and change our image to what it used to be.

> *Give her of the fruit of her hands, and let her works praise her in the gates."*

Proverbs 31.31

For Thought or Discussion

1. The concept of fruit-bearing is an important one throughout scripture. Using Matthew 21.18–19, John 15.1–2, Prov-

erbs 12.14, and Psalm 1.3, what consequences can we expect if we do not bear fruit in our homes?

2. Jesus said of false teachers, "By their fruits you shall know them," a general rule that holds true in every area. What specific fruits should a good homemaker produce and not produce?

3. Discuss the term "dysfunctional family" in regard to this metaphor.

4. "Workers at home" (Titus 2.5) is sometimes translated "keepers at home," indicating a guard. What things must a woman guard her home against?

3. A Help Meet

God saw a need and said, "It is not good that man should be alone; I will make a help meet for him" (Gen 2.18). Notice, that is two words—a help meet, "meet" being the adjective of the word "help." Our modern dictionaries put them together as helpmeet or helpmate and define it as "wife." According to Mr. Webster, every married woman is a "helpmeet," but the Bible usage involves a distinction, specifying what kind of help the woman is to be—a meet help, or as some versions read, "a helper suitable" to the man.

In one sense woman is suitable to man by her very nature, this is, because he "made them male and female" (Matt 19.4). God made man and woman to complement one another in an emotional way as well. Man is the idealist who sets the lofty goals; woman is the pragmatist who pulls them down to something within reach and organizes the process of getting there. Man is the strong one who goes out to deal with the world; woman is the softer one who soothes his wounds. Man is the cynic who, as such, is able to protect his family from those who might take advantage of them; woman is the more merciful one, who sometimes allows it to excuse faults or wrongs that need punishing. Together they temper one another and are more than they could ever be apart.

But in another real sense, not every woman is suitable to every man. We would do well to teach our children this fact. They grow up believing in "happily ever after" and "love conquers all," but after years of picking up muddy boots and strewn clothes, listening to foul language or crude habits, and waking up at 2:00 a.m. with no idea where he is, she begins to wonder if her love has enough ammunition left to conquer anything else. We must teach them to be more objective—more cold-blooded—about choosing a mate.

What about his chosen career? It takes a completely different kind of woman to be a doctor's wife than to be a farmer's wife; to be a policeman's wife than to be a small business owner's wife. Each job carries demands on the man that will affect his family. Sometimes he will be called away at a moment's notice. Sometimes he will be in danger. Sometimes he will need to keep things confidential. Sometimes she may need to pitch in and work right next to him. Can you handle it? If you haven't thought of these things before your marriage, if you haven't discussed the problems that could arise, you have been short-sighted at best and foolish at worst.

But once a woman has taken the plunge, if she is not suited to him, it becomes her duty to make herself suitable to her man, even if it means changing lifelong habits and ideas. When I recognize a problem, it becomes my responsibility to try to solve it whether anyone else helps or not (Rom 2.6). If

I see my marriage faltering because of our differences, I need to do everything I can to repair the situation. And most men are not as bad as some women would have us believe. When he sees such obvious efforts on his wife's part, the husband usually works harder himself; but even if he doesn't, shirking responsibilities will not be excused.

Changing will be easier if she is optimistic and open-minded. If she goes into something dreading it, thinking she will hate it, griping at every little thing that does not suit her, then 99% of the time, she *will* hate it. And what's more, so will he. He will come away dissatisfied, and she will wonder why because after all "we did just what he wanted." For example, in choosing a vacation trip, where they went or what they did was less the point than having a good time—with her! Her dissatisfaction and complaining made them both miserable.

Try approaching things with a positive attitude, determined to find something in them you can enjoy, and equally determined not to gripe. Does it require physical exertion? Look at it as a way to improve your health. Is he much better at it than you? Look at it as a way to build his ego. Compliment him fervently and he will become a gallant knight right before your eyes. (When was the last time you gave him a real compliment anyway?) Is it "just not the way you are?" Then use it to improve your self-discipline (2 Pet 1.6). None of us have enough. Will it mess up your hairdo? (Yes, I have actually heard that one!) Really now, your companionship does a whole lot more for your marriage than your hairdo.

"It is not good that the man should be alone." Make yourself meet, suitable, for him.

There is another angle to this help business. The very word demands that the woman not be a hindrance. How many times have you heard it said of a man, "He'd be a good _____ if it weren't for his wife?" Especially in regard to his spiritual duties, what could your husband be if you were a better person? A personal worker? A Bible class teacher? A full-time gospel preacher? A deacon? An elder? Perhaps he needs to develop himself more as well, but will he do so if he knows that all he will get from you is derision and criticism of his efforts or complaints about the time his new duties take or, worse yet, if he knows your character does not fit the bill (1 Tim 3.11)? Won't you feel ashamed if your husband has to tell the Lord, "I have married a wife and therefore I cannot come" (Luke 14.20)?

Be a help to the man you love, not a hindrance; a steppingstone on his way to Heaven, not a stumbling block over which he plunges straight into Hell. And make no mistake about it. If that's what happens, you will be there too.

> *Do nothing from rivalry or conceit, but in humility count others more significant than yourselves. Let each of you look not only to his [or her] own interests, but also to the interests of others.*
>
> Philippians 2.3–4

For Thought or Discussion

1. Find various translations of Genesis 2.18. Discuss the meaning of the word "meet" and its implications.

2. Does the idea of "complementing" one another necessarily mean that "opposites attract" or will make a successful marriage?

3. Do some research into marriage books and what they have to say about "opposites attract."

4. Trying to change to be "meet" for our men can engender resentment. Why, and what can we do to overcome this?

5. Discuss these Bible women as "helpers:" Elizabeth (Luke 1), Priscilla (Acts 18 and Romans 16), Job's wife (Job 2), Solomon's wives (Neh 13.23–27).

4. A Crown to Her Husband

A worthy woman is a crown to her husband, but she that makes ashamed is as rottenness in his bones. (Prov 12.4)

A crown shows that a man is a leader, worthy of respect and honor. A wife crowns or dethrones her husband with her spoken attitudes and behavior. The public often takes its cue from her, for who can respect a "man who knows not how to rule his own house?" (1 Tim 3.5).

His wife's subjection is probably the surest gauge of a husband's character. Despite all her protestations, a wife who is not in subjection is easy to spot—she will not be in subjection anywhere. In Bible classes she is controversial, opinionated, and pushy. She speaks her mind in a sarcastic, hostile, or offensive tone of voice—and woe to the teacher who tries to point this out! She makes public scenes either by raising her voice or by being careless of who may be within earshot. Any man, anywhere, any time is prey to her razor-sharp tongue.

A wife's loyalty to her husband is another way of bestowing honor on him. Unfortunately, we who consider ourselves loyal may behave in disloyal ways without ever realizing it. Loyalty is not confined to sexual fidelity.

A woman who does things she and her friends know her husband disapproves of is disloyal. Do you have to hide things from him? The phone bill? The credit card statement? Do you keep a dress for six months so that when you finally whip it out and wear it you can "truthfully" say, "No this isn't new. I've had it quite awhile." You might be surprised at some of the things I have heard women admit to. Even if his demands are unreasonable, the very fact that you gripe about them to others and then disregard them, shows that you want others to feel the same disdain for him you do. God intended that a husband and wife be *for* each other, each the one the other can count on.

A gossiping wife causes others to think less of her husband. How much would you be willing to share with a man whose wife spent half her day on the phone—or the internet? Would you go to him for help with a problem? Would you be inclined to "confess your faults" (Jas 5.16)? Gossip causes everyone to "wag their heads" (Psa 64.8), a sure sign of disrespect.

A wife surely demeans her husband by making statements that begin, "He knows better than to…" as if he should fear the consequences she might hand out. What tales we tell about our marriages without realizing it!

Immoral behavior is probably the greatest disgrace a wife can bring to her husband. It leaves others questioning not only his control of the home, but his manhood as well.

More Christians slip into adultery than you want to believe. Others get as close to it as they can with their choice of clothing. Lewd dress encourages men to think thoughts about other men's wives that they have no business thinking. Not only has she shamed her husband, but she has caused others to sin as well.

When a woman acts in these ways, she is telling the world, "I do not feel my husband is worthy of honor and respect. Why should you?" And that publicly expressed attitude, even if never spoken aloud, eats away at him: "but she who makes ashamed is as rottenness in his bones." Just as cancer can kill the body, a wife can murder her husband's spirit.

Respect your husband; honor him as head. Do nothing that will shame him. Be a crown, the reason others respect and honor him. As it is said of the worthy woman:

> *Her husband is known in the gates where he sits among the elders of the land.*
>
> Proverbs 31.23

For Thought or Discussion

1. Besides those listed above, come up with other examples of showing disrespect to a husband.

2. Showing respect is just as important in the home as out of it. Why?

3. Husbands occasionally need correcting. How should that be done? Find Bible examples, good and bad.

4. Several men are mentioned in the Bible only because of their wives. See how many you can find. What did her actions say about him?

5. Discuss Proverbs 14.1 in regard to this metaphor.

5. Worth More than Rubies

We've already quoted from Proverbs 31 extensively—the worthy woman, or as the King James reads, the virtuous woman. Maybe it's worth checking out the meaning of "worthy." Just what makes this woman so rare and precious, her value "far above rubies?" The word itself has a depth of meaning you might never suspect.

The Hebrew word for worthy or virtuous, *chayil,* is used 150 times in the Old Testament. Look at these other words it is often translated by: army, band of men, band of soldiers, company, forces, great forces, host, might, power, strength, substance, valor, war, able, strong, and valiant. Look up these passages where the word is translated by one of those: Judges 21.10; 1 Samuel 9.1; 14.48; 2 Kings 2.16; 1 Chronicles 5.18; 2 Chronicles 33.14. Of the 150 available, that is a good representation. Can you find the word in those verses? If you see one that has anything to do with brave, strong men, that's it:"worthy."

We tend to think of strength and courage as specifically masculine traits, and yes, men may have the monopoly on brute strength, but look through Proverbs 31. Not only does this woman have the strength to survive long, busy days, one after the other with no end in sight, but she has the inner strength to survive life! "Hothouse flowers" who "have the vapors" are not who God had in mind when he created woman.

A woman should have the strength to stand by a man through thick and thin, "in sickness and in health, for better or for worse" and all the other things she promised all those years ago; to manage her household (1 Tim 5.14), to teach her children, to help the needy, to serve the saints, and "to stand against the wiles of the Devil," and to "quench all the fiery darts of the Evil One" (Ephesians 6.11,16).

By using this word "worthy" in Proverbs 31, both at the beginning of the passage (v 10) and at the end (v 29), God is surely telling us that he expects his women to be strong, inside and out. She won't wilt when times get rough, when one trial after the other besets her soul.

She won't leave when the money is so scarce she can't go shopping with the girls, when all the appliances break down at once and she can't afford new ones. She might even have to put her hands in dishwater and scrub, or hang clothes on a clothesline in the winter, but she will do whatever is necessary, when it is necessary.

She won't go to pieces when the schedule is full and time is short, when there is a deadline to meet and being late is not an option.

She doesn't have to have a certain brand, a certain level of living, a certain status among her peers or "my life is ruined."

She will stand by a man, even when he makes mistakes that he has to pay for with shame and humility, forgiving and comforting as only someone intimately close can.

She will not only stand by her husband, but stand up for the Lord, even when it means losing friends and making enemies, possibly even among her spiritual brethren. She won't give up on the Lord because others have made a mockery of their own faith.

In all these areas and more, she plays the hand she was dealt and comes away a winner.

Ladies, God says there is strength and courage in femininity—don't let anyone tell you otherwise.

> *A **worthy** [strong, valiant] woman, who can find? Her price is far above rubies; she girds her loins with strength, and makes her arms strong. Strength and dignity are her clothing and she laughs at the time to come. Many daughters have done **valiantly** but you excel them all. Give her of the fruit of her hands, and let her works praise her in the gates.*
>
> Proverbs 31.10, 17, 25, 29, 31

For Thought or Discussion

1. How does the idea of being "strong" directly oppose the me-centered culture we live in today?

2. Look at the fruit of the Spirit in Galatians 5.22–23. How does each element relate to strength?

3. Read the story of Rizpah in 2 Samuel 21.1–14. How did this woman show enormous strength, physically, emotionally, and spiritually?

4. Find other examples of feminine strength in the scriptures, and apply them to today.

6. Desire of the Eyes

In Ezekiel 24.16, Jehovah refers to Ezekiel's wife as "the desire of your eyes." Too many wives miss the significance of that description. We think that once we have caught ourselves a man, we don't have to worry about our appearance. If this verse means anything, it means that Ezekiel loved to look at his wife, that her appearance pleased him. That doesn't just happen. In some manner, she paid enough attention to herself to stay attractive to him.

That verse also says a lot about Ezekiel. *She* was the desire of his eyes, no one else. *She* was the one he wanted to look at, not every other woman who might display herself in an inappropriate way. He wasn't in the market for another woman. Notice also, Ezekiel was thirty when the book began, and no more than 36 when it ended. He was not an older man with a decreased libido. To even a young Ezekiel there was one woman and one woman only.

But that still doesn't take away from the idea that a godly woman is careful about her appearance. I am not going to tell you that you have to stay a size 4—if you ever were to begin with. Carrying his children and preparing his meals, plus the added responsibility of hospitality that in the Scriptures always involves sharing a meal, precludes any notion of a girl-like figure lasting through fifty years of marriage. I am, however, supposed to be a living sacrifice (Rom 12.1). That means I take care of my health as surely as it meant keeping those animal sacrifices healthy and unblemished. It means I exercise self-control in all things (Gal 5.23; 2 Pet 1.6). I heard one woman say, "To lose weight I have to be hungry, and I just won't do that." With that attitude, Jesus would have turned the stones into a four course meal.

Yet even the most conscientious of women put it on. Unless you are genetically predisposed to thinness, there comes a time when either your metabolism has slowed too much with age or you are under activity restrictions for medical reasons which make it more difficult to exercise it off. Discouragement is constant. Men can leave the butter off their bread and lose ten pounds in a month. You can leave out both the butter and the bread, and maybe you will lose half a pound that month, but you will gain it and four more back the next weekend when you have company or cook for a church potluck. You simply accept that your waistline will thicken, and a good man will understand. But a Christian always exercises moderation and self-control, and always cares for her Temple (1 Cor 6.19–20), even a slightly larger one.

But if your figure is the only thing that makes you the desire of your husband's eyes, you obviously picked the wrong man. Watching your weight is only a small part of a woman's appearance and, except in cases endangering health, probably the most superficial. A lot can be said for just staying presentable. Are you clean and sweet-smelling? Is your hair clean and combed? Are your clothes clean, pressed, and mended? It is just as impossible to live with a woman and never see her in curlers and cold cream as it is to live with a man and never see him sweaty and unshaven, but is she still shuffling around in those dingy scuffs and that ratty terrycloth robe at noon? Does she save her nice clothes, makeup, and hairdos for others, and always wear holey jeans or frumpy house dresses and leave her hair scraggly and un-kempt for him, even when it isn't window-washing, bean-picking, or floor-scrubbing day?

The worthy woman made "for herself carpets of tapes-try, her clothing is fine linen and purple" (Prov 31.22). We certainly do not advocate living beyond one's means, but the wife should make some effort to look nice—for him. It costs more time and money than most of us have to look glamor-ous, but just a little time and effort would give some hus-bands a welcome change, plenty enough for him to call her "the desire of my eyes."

The most important way for women to stay beautiful is to "adorn themselves in modest apparel, with shamefast-ness and sobriety, not with braided hair and gold or pearls, but (which becomes women professing godliness) with good works" (1 Tim 2.9–10). Many a plain woman has be-come beautiful to me as I came to know her because of her character shining through, but no amount of makeup has hidden for long the ugliness of others.

One cannot make her features more regular or remove the flaws from her skin, but she can clean up her soul and with God's help, keep it white as snow. She can keep from becoming hard and bitter. She can keep her voice from screeching and whinng. She can keep her face from scowling and sneering.

A man has no business expecting his fifty-year old wife to look twenty-five, but he has every reason to expect her character to grow younger until she becomes "as a little child" (Mark 10.15). As the king advised in Proverbs 31.30, "Grace is deceitful and beauty is vain, but a woman who fears Jehovah, she shall be praised."

> *Let your adorning be the hidden person of the heart with the imperishable beauty of a gentle and quiet spirit, which in God's sight is very precious.*
>
> 1 Peter 3.4

For Thought or Discussion

1. Why does this subject instantly raise the hackles on most women? Is the concept presented here a valid one?

2. When can "keeping your figure" get in the way of spiritual interests and obligations?

3. What attributes of a Christian are involved in keeping this area of our lives in proper balance?

4. How is this the perfect example of not "judging by appearance" (John 7.24)?

5. What do we need to teach our sons in regard to judging a woman's beauty?

7. The Weaker Vessel

Likewise, husbands, live with your wives in an understanding way, showing honor to the woman as the weaker vessel, since they are heirs with you of the grace of life, so that your prayers may not be hindered. (1 Peter 3.7)

The concept of "vessel" as figurative of bodies, lives, even nations, has been well established since Old Testament times (1 Sam 21.4–5; Psa 31.12; Isa 65.4; Jer 18). The figure is continued in the New Testament in passages such as Acts 9.15, 2 Corinthians 4.7, Romans 9.19ff, 2 Timothy 2.20–21, as well as the passage above. In both the Hebrew and Greek the word literally means "utensil" or "instrument." One scholar says that in 1 Peter the word "woman" should be an adjective: "…giving honor unto the *womanly* vessel…" as opposed to the manly vessel. In other words, the man is an instrument too, and both man and woman are instruments of God, not one of the other, "joint-heirs of the grace of life."

I read an article once using the metaphor of crystal goblets and Mason jars. Which is the weaker (more fragile) vessel? Yet which one is treated with the most honor (care, protection)? In many societies the men have used their greater strength to take advantage of the women, using them as workhorses, and ignoring their needs. When I was younger I heard a man say, "In my day, women used to have babies and go out and work in the field the next day." My husband replied, "And a lot more of them died young too." It has only been in modern civilization that the average lifespan of women has surpassed that of men. A good many of the laws that seem slanted against women in the Old Testament, were actually given for their protection. The scriptures teach that men are not to take advantage of women just because of their greater physical strength but to give them the honor and care of a fragile, crystal goblet.

Some have a problem with the word "weaker." The word does not mean "weak." It is a word of comparison. It means "less strong," and it certainly does not apply to intellect or emotion. As we recently discovered, the woman of Proverbs 31 possesses the strength to handle life's problems instead of being another emotional burden on her husband. A man wants a woman who can keep her head in a crisis, bear disappointment with a smile, and take heartbreak without a complete collapse. And yes, it is right for him to want a woman who can and *will* work alongside him without complaining.

I have dug ditches in a monsoon next to my husband to keep our house from washing away. But he sent me in after the worst was done, to rest and dry off while he "just finished up," another hour's work. There are times when things must be done and one has to muster up as much physical strength as possible, but the strongest man is still stronger than the strongest woman. Until all athletic contests are no longer gender specific and the women are regularly winning, there is no denying that men are physically stronger.

The media consistently presents the man of the family as a buffoon, a bumbling idiot who must always be saved from himself by his far more intelligent, cultured, sensible wife. Even the Berenstain Bears children's books picture Papa bear that way! Do you think I haven't heard Christian women talk about their men in exactly the same manner?

God designed the man to be the provider and protector (1 Tim 5.8; Gen 3.17–19), even to giving his life for his wife if necessary (Eph 5.25). *Let him use what God put in him!* Nowadays we are so civilized that we seldom need any real protection—no wild animals, no angry natives; men no longer have any dramatic way to prove themselves. Then, to make it worse, we steal our husbands' self-esteem by complaining about the standard of living he has provided, laughing at his attempts to buy us gifts, and insulting his careful planning for our financial security. If you don't think you are being treated with the honor you deserve, maybe it's because you have not let him honor you in the only ways he knows how, the ways God programmed into him.

It is up to you to let your husband be the head of the house. Ephesians 5.22 never tells the husband to put his wife into subjection. In the same way, he cannot "nourish and cherish" you (literally "feed and warm") if you do not let him (Eph 5.29). God used marriage as a pattern for his relationship with His people. He had a problem when his "wife" went to someone besides Him for her needs and her protection, and when she insisted that she could take care of herself without Him (Hos 2.5–13). What makes us think a man will feel any differently when we act like we don't need him?

> *But if any provide not for his own, and specially his own house-hold, he hath denied the faith, and is worse than an unbeliever.*
>
> 1 Timothy 5.8

For Thought or Discussion

1. How does understanding the use of the word "woman" and the ownership of the vessel (first paragraph) help protect women?

2. What everyday actions of ours can deny our men the instinctual role of provider and protector?

3. What small things can we do to build them up?

4. What is the problem in our attitudes when we allow descriptions like "the weaker vessel" and "the help" to cause resentment?

5. In what ways were these women strong without denying the greater physical strength of the men involved: Deborah (Jdg 4); Mary (Matt 1; 2.19–23; John 19.26–27)?

8. A Cistern

Drink waters out of your own cistern, And running waters out of your own well. Should your springs be dispersed abroad, And streams of water in the streets? Let them be for yourself alone, And not for strangers with you. Let your fountain be blessed; And rejoice in the wife of your youth. As a loving hind and a pleasant doe, Let her breasts satisfy you at all times; And be ravished always with her love. (Prov 5.15–19)

In many ladies' Bible class books on marriage, especially those written by women, any reference to the sexual relationship is either absent or barely skimmed over. Obviously, no one is comfortable with this topic, and maybe that is why more and more marriages are falling apart due to adultery. God had a plan for marriage, and when we neglect any part of that plan, it will not be the perfect plan He created.

The passage above from Proverbs is not only beautiful, but plainly written and instructive if we do more than read through it quickly with our eyes cast down in embarrassment.

"Drink waters from your *own* cistern, and running water out of your *own* well." Yes, there is a possessiveness that is

right in a marriage, just as God, who depicted his relationship with his people as a marriage, said, "I am a jealous God."
I have every right to expect my husband to be mine and mine
alone, and he has every right to expect the same from me. In
fact, we each have the right to expect that we were the only
ones *ever*. "For this is the will of God…that you should ab-
stain from fornication…that no man defraud his brother…"
(1 Thes 4.3–6). When I give myself to another man before
marriage, I have defrauded my future husband of what is
rightfully his and his alone, and the same holds true for men.
God is an equal opportunity God.

"Should your springs be dispersed abroad, and streams of
water in the streets? Let them be for yourself alone and not
for strangers with you." The physical relationship between a
husband and wife is not only intimate, it is private, not for
general consumption, and sacred in that privacy. "Let marriage be held in honor and the marriage bed undefiled," the
Hebrew writer adds in 13.4. This part of the relationship is
too precious to be thrown into the street for just anyone to
see or hear about.

"Let your fountain be blessed…" The fountain here is a
parallelism for the cistern, a deep well hewn out of rock. In
the scriptures "cistern" is symbolic of many things, including a necessity of life in a home (Deut 6.11), a peaceful and
comfortable home (2 Kgs 18.31), and a source of life (Isa
51.1). Those are more than appropriate descriptions in this
case where the cistern and fountain symbolize the woman's
body. If the fountain is "blessed," a Hebrew word that is of-

ten translated "happy," it becomes obvious that the woman is neither abused nor does she dislike the sexual aspect of marriage. That is emphasized further when the writer continues, "Rejoice in the wife of your youth." This relationship is a joyful one. When Abimelech looked out his window and saw the "brother and sister" team of Isaac and Rebekah "sporting" (Gen 26.7–9), two things became apparent to him. First, they were married. Despite the culture we live in, there are things that a husband and wife do that unmarried couples do *not* do. Second, they were both enjoying what was going on. Ladies, not only does God expect you to enjoy this part of your marriage, it can ruin it for the man you say you love if you do not.

"In the wife of your youth," the writer says. I found a commentator who said that could correctly be translated, "whom you married in your youth." In other words, they are no longer young, but they are still together. God designed marriage for one man and one woman for one lifetime. He designed this aspect of marriage the same way. This couple in Proverbs is no longer young but they are still enjoying the sexual relationship God designed. Frequency and intensity may change, but the need for intimacy in a marriage never goes away. If you find yourself married to a man you no longer know, maybe it's because you amputated part of the relationship a long time ago.

"Let her breasts satisfy you at all times." This husband, despite his wife's advancing age, is content with what he has. We have already spoken about keeping yourself desirable to him as much as possible. But even as your outer beauty fades, you can keep him happy and content by giving him what he needs and wants, when he needs it and wants it.

> But because of the temptation to sexual immorality, each man should have his own wife and each woman her own husband. The husband should give to his wife her conjugal rights, and likewise the wife to her husband. For the wife does not have authority over her own body, but the husband does. Likewise the husband does not have authority over his own body, but the wife does. Do not deprive one another, except perhaps by agreement for a limited time, that you may devote yourselves to prayer; but then come together again, so that Satan may not tempt you because of your lack of self-control. (1 Cor 7.2–5)

This passage does *not* say, "You are mine; I can do with you what I want." What it *does* say is, "I am yours; I will do what you want." The obligation is on the giver not the taker. Too many women do not understand the real need that God has placed in a man's body. Testosterone makes him more aggressive, which enhances his desire to protect you. It also makes him more easily aroused sexually. When you fill that need, it helps to cement the relationship he has with you and his desire to protect and provide for his family. If you do not allow him to fulfill that need in this godly manner, not only can you damage the relationship, you may be responsible for causing him to stumble (sin), and God *will* hold you accountable. The Hebrew word for cistern (*bor*) is sometimes used of a dungeon or prison—a deep one. When a man is locked into a sexless marriage, he is in a very real prison, one where he is tempted almost beyond endurance every day of his life, but unable to get out of it and stay faithful to the God he also made that marriage covenant before. Yes, God allows for a time of abstinence to "devote yourself to prayer." Most of the enforced abstinence I know of happens because she got mad and wanted to punish him, not so she could pray. Ladies, you are playing with fire when you do this, and you may just get burned—eternally.

"Be ravished always with her love." Imagine my surprise when I discovered that the word translated "ravished" means to be deceived or to go astray. What? I thought confusedly. Then I got it. He is so enraptured, enamored, entranced, and captivated by her that he simply loses his good sense. Like a man who is intoxicated, he wants no one but her, and she is on his mind day and night. If you have a man who treats you like that, it can be the most erotic thing in the world. Most of us are not beautiful in the world's eyes, nor glamorous; but a man who treats you like you are is all any woman really needs. Now you give him what he needs. Don't make him beg. Don't make him miserable.

Treat him like the love of your life, the man who provides and protects to the best of his ability and wants nothing more than to be with you and you alone forever.

As an apple tree among the trees of the forest, so is my beloved among the young men. With great delight I sat in his shadow, and his fruit was sweet to my taste. He brought me to the banqueting house, and his banner over me was love. Sustain me with raisins; refresh me with apples, for I am sick with love. His left hand is under my head, and his right hand embraces me! ... The voice of my beloved! Behold, he comes, leaping over the mountains, bounding over the hills. My beloved is like a gazelle or a young stag. Behold, there he stands behind our wall, gazing through the windows, looking through the lattice. My beloved speaks and says to me: ...Arise, my love, my beautiful one, and come away. O my dove, in the clefts of the rock, in the crannies of the cliff, let me see your face, let me hear your voice, for your voice is sweet, and your face is lovely. ...My beloved is mine, and I am his.

Song of Solomon 2.3–6, 8–9, 13–14, 16

For Thought or Discussion:

1. What should we be teaching our children about fornication that is seldom said (1 Thes 4.3–6)?

2. What are wrong, or simply unwise, things to teach our daughters about the sexual relationship in marriage?

3. What is the difference between denying sexual favors and being physically unable to perform due to illness or disability?

4. Why is denying sexual favors to one's husband spiritually dangerous to both?

5. Fill in the blank with as many items as you think fit: when it comes to the sexual relationship in her marriage, a woman should never _____.

9. Companion of Your Youth

Yet you say, Wherefore? Because Jehovah has been witness between you and the wife of your youth, against whom you have dealt treacherously, though she is your companion. (Mal 2.14)

The Hebrew word for "companion" in this passage, *chaber*, is the feminine form, used only here. The masculine form is used in Judges 20.11, "So all the men of Israel were gathered against the city, *knit together* as one man." "Knit together" is the word "companion" and that spells out exactly how close God expects us to be as companions to our husbands, two threads, one cloth.

Malachi obviously speaks to older men who were "dealing treacherously" with the women they had married young, trading them in on a new model, as we often say nowadays. They had forgotten the covenant they made when they were younger to be a companion, not just for awhile, but for life. Men are not the only ones who need this reminder. "So you will be delivered from… the adulteress with her smooth words, who forsakes the friend of her youth and forgets the covenant of her God" (Prov 2.16–17).

The English word the translators chose, "companion," originally derived from "someone to share bread with." It speaks of a closeness beyond simple acquaintance. When people put their feet under the same table, they learn far more about each other than they ever will with a hand-shake in the foyer. For a man and woman to share a meal, the assumption is intimacy. What do you think of a couple you see eating together in a restaurant? Either they are married or dating.

The intimacy of a marriage, of course, goes far beyond eating together. When I see a man whose tie is askew or whose collar is turned up, I tell his wife. I would never put my hands on another woman's husband in quite that way. In the same manner, Keith and I eat off one another's plates and share drinks, we brush lint off one another, and get in one another's personal space without a second thought. The sexual relationship, which we have already discussed (see "Cistern"), is a natural element of male-female companion-ship and all these small nuances are its natural byproducts. That is why married people should be careful who they spend the most time with.

God meant that this companionship begin, ideally, in youth, and continue for a lifetime. "A man shall leave his father and mother and shall cleave to his wife" (Gen 2.24). As he reaches manhood, as she reaches womanhood, they search out a companion, make a covenant together and begin a marriage. In their "youth," however a particular culture may define it, they learn together and grow together. They make plans and share a purpose—together. These choices they make, not some overpowering feeling they cannot control. Choosing to be together and using that time to best effect makes the relationship more and more intimate as the years go by. But just as the myth with children, "quality time" does not happen if a quantity of time is not being spent at it. Anything that lessens companionship, in both quality and quantity, is a danger to the relationship.

Dating couples need to be talking about these things early on. If you cannot agree on life goals, if you do not share priorities, if you become bored in one another's company, this is not the ideal companion for you. Stop now before you get in so deep you feel unable to get out. It will only make the hurt worse to continue in something that will have no good end. You are talking about a lifetime decision here, one that will affect you as no other will, one that can even determine your eternity.

It is interesting that Barnes defines "companion" as "another self." While some time alone can be re-invigorating to a marriage, it should always leave one with a sense that something is missing. Couples who make it a habit to be away from one another are lessening that sense of belonging. "But we've grown apart," some will say to excuse divorce, condemning themselves in the process. The whole point of the relationship is togetherness—"knit together." Do we think this happens by magic? If we have "grown apart," we have been raveling instead of knitting. It is our responsibility to make sure we grow closer together. That does not mean that we must share every single interest, but we should share the things that matter the most.

When you've started out young and made it together through the various trials of life, the relationship grows stronger, deeper, and sweeter. Knowing there is always someone you can count on, that any little tiff will soon be over and all will be right again, gives you a sense of security that will see you through the toughest times, and that includes the time when this lifetime relationship is broken by death. To hear my mother say to my father just moments before he died, "Wait for me at the gate. I'll be there soon," was something I will cherish till my time comes to say the same words. That is what companionship is all about.

From those first baby steps as a brand new person—"one flesh"—to the maturity of an interdependent couple who have seen the both the best and the worst of each other, who have helped each other, supported each other, lived together, worked together, laughed together and cried together—a married couple should cling to one another and no one else in this relationship, under the loving watch of the Father who designed it.

And God said, "It is not good for man to be alone."

Genesis 2.18

For Thought or Discussion

1. Discuss the old saying, "Absence makes the heart grow fonder," in relationship to the companionship of marriage.

2. In what ways does companionship stabilize a marriage?

3. What sorts of specific companionship are absolutely necessary to a marriage?

4. Name some things that can legitimately cause separation between spouses and ways to keep the companionship going in those situations.

5. How can these things be a danger to companionship—careers, hobbies, children?

10. Covenant Partner

And this second thing you do. You cover the LORD's altar with tears, with weeping and groaning because he no longer regards the offering or accepts it with favor from your hand. But you say, "Why does he not?" Because the LORD was witness between you and the wife of your youth, to whom you have been faithless, though she is your companion and your wife by covenant. Did he not make them one, with a portion of the Spirit in their union? And what was the one God seeking? Godly offspring. So guard yourselves in your spirit, and let none of you be faithless to the wife of your youth. "For the man who does not love his wife but divorces her, says the LORD, the God of Israel, covers his garment with violence, says the LORD of hosts. So guard yourselves in your spirit, and do not be faithless." (Mal 2.13–16)

The passage in Malachi also reminds us that the husband and wife are covenant partners, which is the last and perhaps most important description of a wife we will discuss. No other passage in the Bible brings home the seriousness of breaking that covenant in quite the same way.

The one who does this is "faithless" (vv 15–16). In another

version he is called "treacherous." A covenant partner has every right to feel secure in that relationship. Even a con man like Laban recognized that God was the witness in a marriage covenant (Gen 31.49–50), and even in a polygamous culture, lines were drawn. As we learned earlier, faithlessness was not confined to men (Prov 2.17). Women can forsake men just as easily, especially these days when "I am woman!" seems to be a call to independence away from men and family in general.

Malachi states plainly that breaking the marriage covenant is considered "violence" (v 16), and as above in Genesis 31, "oppression." The violence may not be physical, but anyone who has seen the heartbreak of a divorce knows that the "tears" and "groans" (v 13), are just as real and inflict just as much damage. I have seen forsaken husbands and wives alike practically disintegrate before my eyes, losing weight, and aging ten years in a month. God will hold the one who causes that "violence" to His child accountable.

If nothing else brings home the gravity of violating a covenant, perhaps this will: God will no longer accept the offering of one who breaks the marriage covenant (v 13), and s/he no longer has the Spirit (v 15). For anyone who still has any recognition at all of his need for the grace of God and the help and comfort of the Holy Spirit in his life, this should be terrifying. It should certainly be a wake-up call for all those who think they can still be a Christian after dissolving the covenant they swore to for anything other than the one exception Jesus made in Matthew 19.

Malachi reinforces God's displeasure by repeating "thus says the Lord" at the beginning and end of the same sentence (v 16). It is as if God says, "This is what I say…and I mean it!" All through the scriptures, God approaches marriage and its responsibilities as a choice we make voluntarily, but which then makes us responsible to its sacred promises. "Love your husband." "Love your wife." "Respect your husband." "Live joyfully with the wife [spouse] of your youth." If these things just "happened" God would not hold us liable. He expects us to choose to make them happen, working at it, praying for it, fulfilling our individual duties without blaming the other party for the things we refused to do because "the spark has died." God expects me to get out my flint and strike a new one. "It ain't over till it's over," and that isn't until the other party leaves altogether.

Our culture may not honor marriage, considering it as breakable as an athlete's contract, but "from the beginning it was not so," Jesus said in Matthew 19. One man, one woman, one lifetime—that's what God intended. A marriage is not between two persons, but three. God is that third partner. When you stand there in that beautiful white gown thinking this day is all about you, remember Who Else you are making a vow to. Even if someday you think so little of your spouse that you would break a solemn oath to him, think twice before you break it to a Creator who could destroy you with a thought.

> *When you shall vow a vow unto Jehovah your God, you shall not be slack to pay it: for Jehovah your God will surely require it of you; and **it would be sin in you**. That which is gone out*

of your lips you shall observe and do; according as you have vowed unto Jehovah your God.

Deuteronomy 23.21, 23

Live joyfully *with the wife [or husband] whom you love* **all the days of your life**_of vanity, which he has given you under the sun, all your days of vanity: for that is your portion in life, and in your labor wherein you labor under the sun.*

Ecclesiastes 9.9

For Thought or Discussion

1. Do some research into the elements of a covenant in the ancient world.

2. What does Jesus say about oaths and vows in general and what bearing does that have on our marriage vows?

3. Find as many divorces in the Bible as you can. Do any of them have God's seal of approval?

4. What is wrong with the notion that two people who had the right to marry in the first place can "just live apart and as long as we don't remarry we are okay?"

5. Do a quick review of the descriptions we have covered and what they mean to a marriage.

Also by Dene Ward

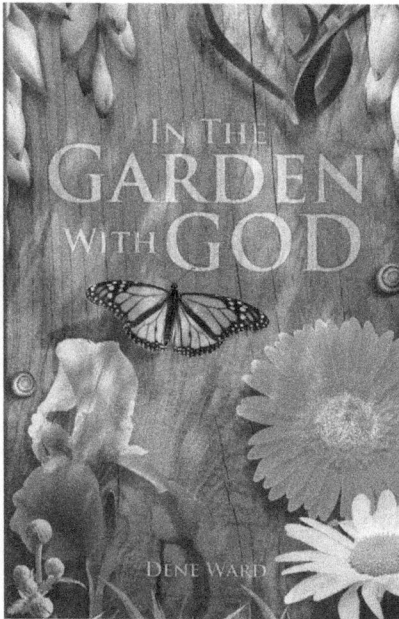

In the Garden with God

Dene Ward and her husband Keith have gardened for nearly 40 years, which has shown her why God's prophets and preachers, including Jesus, used so many references to plants and planting—it's only natural. Join her for a walk in the garden with God. 142 pages. $9.99 (PB)

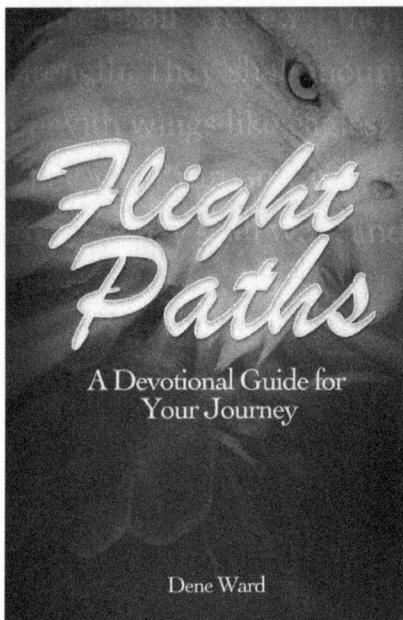

Flight Paths
A Devotional Guide for your Journey

When encroaching blindness took her music teaching career away, Dene Ward turned her attention to writing. What began as e-mail devotions to some friends grew into a list of hundreds of subscribers. Three hundred sixty-six of those devotions have been assembled to form this daily devotional. Follow her through a year of camping, bird-watching, medical procedures, piano lessons, memories, and more as she uses daily life as a springboard to thought-provoking and character-challenging messages of endurance and faith. 475 pages. $18.99 (PB)

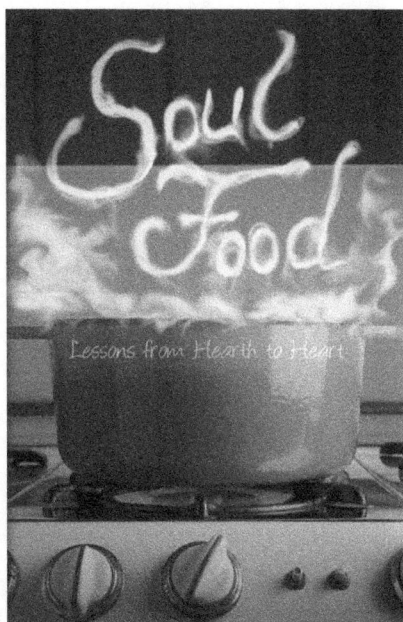

Soul Food
Lessons from Hearth to Heart

Cooking has always been a part of Dene Ward's life. She grew up in a house where they were always feeding someone and followed that same path as a wife and mother. On the table, she has always offered a nourishing meal; she now offers this collection to feed your souls, lessons from her hearth to your heart. 148 pages. $9.99 (PB)

For a full listing of our books, visit DeWard's website:
www.deward.com